"Believe in yourself! Have faith in your abilities!
Without a humble but reasonable confidence in your own
powers you cannot be successful or happy."

"Change your thoughts and you change your world."

Norman Vincent Peale
Author of *Think and Grow Rich*

How To Find
True Love

Love is the greatest force
in the Universe, and with
your thoughts you can
create True Love.

You deserve to be loved
for who you Truely are,

Love + faith,
Blenda Pilon

How To Find True Love

CHANGE YOUR THOUGHTS
CHANGE YOUR RELATIONSHIPS

BLENDA R. PILON, MSc
Author of LOVE SECRETS,
Falling in Love & Staying in Love

DISCLAIMER

As long as you consistantly follow the instructions under the section entitled What You Need to Know in *HOW TO FIND TRUE LOVE,* you will be successful in finding True Love. If this is not your experience, then upon the return of your book, the purchase price of your book will be refunded to you.

ISBN Paperback: 978-1-7753897-0-5
ISBN eBook: 978-1-7753897-1-2

Cover artwork: Germancreative - Fiverr
Interior design: Ghislain Viau

*This book is dedicated to all those people
who desire True Love
and are willing to work for it!
You Can Do It!*

Acknowledgements

I acknowledge and thank my friends and associates
who shared their ideas and helped me with
editing and layout including my husband,
Rev. Raymond Pilon, Raywyn Erikson, Bonnie Dixon,
Amanda Rallings, Dr. Melba Burns, Judy Bowers,
and Ghislain Viau.

Introduction

Have you ever been thinking of someone and then suddenly that person is calling you, texting you, or emailing you? Is this supernatural? Is this happening because thoughts travel? Do thoughts create your experiences? By using your thoughts correctly, can you create the loving relationships your heart desires? Can you use your thoughts to activate the Law of Attraction and attract your perfect partner?

Do thoughts form your beliefs? Do you agree with what Napoleon Hill said in **Think and Grow Rich: A Black Choice**, "Whatever the mind can conceive and believe, it can achieve."

What power do you give your thoughts?

The key belief driving this guidebook *HOW TO FIND TRUE LOVE* is *Thoughts Are Things*. Notice that I am not saying that thoughts become things. I believe thoughts travel instantaneously and create things; therefore, I believe that *thoughts are things*. In this case, the *things* you are interested in are relationships. My passion is to provide you with a *proven way* of how to think correctly so you can enjoy the loving relationship your heart desires. You will experience the magic of thoughts instantly causing what you experience.

By thinking correctly you can create a loving relationship. To do otherwise is to commit yourself to a dis-eased, unhealthy relationship – one which handcuffs your love and imprisons you. That is not what I want for you, and my gut tells me this is not what you want either. Right?

I recommend keeping *HOW TO FIND TRUE LOVE* near you at all times. Keep it handy as a reference guide. Whenever you are feeling fear, anger or disappointment regarding a relationship issue, consult with your guidebook – it is your *Trusted Relationship Toolkit*. Find out what belief you have been having that is causing you *dis-comfort,* and replace it with a *New Thought*. Practice your *New Thought* as I have outlined in this manual – practice it until it becomes your new belief attracting to you what you desire.

Think I am asking a lot of you? I am not asking you to do anything that I myself don't practice. Although I have been happily married for 25 years, I continue to keep my manual of *HOW TO FIND TRUE LOVE* in a place where I can easily access it. To me, my marriage is like a garden. It is important that I weed my garden every day preventing the weeds from taking over and giving the flowers the opportunity to blossom in their full beauty.

I will give you an example of one of the weeds I plucked from my garden. Today I wanted more private time to myself and when my husband kept asking me my opinion about different ideas he was exploring, I started feeling resentful. So, I looked up resentment in my trusted toolkit, *HOW TO FIND TRUE LOVE.* It supplied me with the belief I was having, and the *New Thought* to replace it with. It said:

"RESENTMENT

BELIEF: I am indignant and upset about what my partner is doing. I don't believe my partner wants to hear about what is upsetting me. Because I can't change what is happening, I have to put up with it. I will keep my anger to myself even though I know it is unhealthy to repress emotions.

NEW THOUGHT: I am in charge of my feelings and what happens to me. By trusting my partner, I can better understand the situation. I know my partner is willing to listen to my feelings. When we put love and our relationship first, we can share our thoughts and feelings and overcome any obstacle. We faithfully use our *Love Communication* knowledge and exercises."

After my referencing what my manual said about resentment, I shared my pent-up resentful feelings with my husband. He fully understood and said he wanted to help me. He assured me that if I would let him know when I wanted some privacy, he would do everything in his power to make sure I got it.

From my own experience and from the experience of the many, many people who are using these *New Thoughts*, I know they work – they are *proven and insured.* Because I want your *New Thoughts* to work for you, in this manual I guide you on how to effectively use them.

Let's call these *New Thoughts,* new affirmations. Remember, life is an ongoing process. You may discover some new affirmations that are not even in this manual. If this happens, be creative and invent a new affirmation that will work for you. Remember:

Thoughts form habits, and habits create your destiny.

When you do discover new thoughts that are not in your relationship toolkit; please let me know. I want to share your findings with other people. For me, life is all about people helping people. In my case, my passion is being a guide for you to attract and enjoy the best relationship you can imagine. You have the power, *you are the Love Power,* and you can do it. Remember:

Love is the Greatest Force in the Universe,
and You Can Use It!

How To Find True Love and Enjoy Loving Relationships

Change Your Thoughts, Change Your Relationships

"Beliefs are simply repeated thoughts with strong feelings attached to them. A belief is when you have made up your mind, the verdict is in, you've nailed the door shut and thrown away the key, and there is no room for negotiation."
—Rhonda Byrne, "How *The Secret* Changed My Life"

What You Need to Know

Do you harbour some negative beliefs about your partner? If you answer *No*, you likely need to re-examine your answer.

*"Sometimes a **decision** you made when you were a child morphs into a belief that jeopardizes your whole life."*
—Dr. Melba Burns,
author of "Don't Retire, Refire!"

Negative beliefs develop over time. When you have held them for a long while, they become friends who are guiding your life. Sometimes the guidance is conscious and sometimes it is unconscious. Most often you follow the guidance automatically and don't question it. When you stop and take time to examine your beliefs you will undoubtedly find many that are causing you pain - even sabotaging your relationship. Fortunately, you have an opportunity to go back to the negotiating table and have a frank discussion with yourself regarding your decision making.

You, and you alone have the power to change your beliefs by changing your thoughts. Of course, when you change your thoughts you automatically change what is happening in your relationship.

When you go to the negotiating table with a set of handy options (let's call them relationship tools) to assist you, the process of making changes can be fun and exciting. For example, you can try out a n*ew thought* and watch the effect it has on you and your relationship. If you don't like the result, you can go back to the negotiating table and create a different thought – a different outcome. I recall in the book called *The Secret* by the author Rhonda Byrnes, that Michael Bernard Beckwith claims ***"One good positive thought has more power than a thousand negative thoughts."*** That is why one good positive thought replacing an old pattern of beliefs can totally transform your relationship (your marriage) from one that is not working to a relationship (marriage) that is fulfilling and working.

If you are having doubts because you have already been through therapy or read self-help books and your relationship still does not work for you, you deserve to know why. Why are you facing the same issues? The answer is simple and yet profound. In order to make changes that will last, you must change the mental causes. When you don't change the mental cause, the issues will grow bigger as they repeat themselves. For example, many people leave their partner and find another one. They believe this is a good solution for happiness. Unfortunately when the mental causes have not been changed, they soon discover they are again facing the same issues...and usually more devastating. Of course, the reason for this is not the new partner, but rather that the partner making the change has created the same issues.

Remember, wherever you go, you take yourself! Until you change your core beliefs, your relationship issues will only get worse until what is happening becomes so intolerable you want to change. It is as if your issues have a voice of their own warning you to change. When you fail to listen, your stagnant core beliefs will make your life increasing miserable.

For everything that happens in your relationships, there is a causal thought pattern that precedes and maintains your experience. Your consistent thinking patterns, your beliefs, create your experiences. When you really *"get it"* that it is your thought patterns that create your relationship experiences, then you can stop blaming your partner, your relationship, and other people for what you don't like. Instead, by tapping the awesome *Love Power* within yourself, you can take full responsibility for creating a satisfying relationship. Because old destructive thought patterns are attached to your Ego's needs, they may be hiding in disguise below the level of your conscious awareness. To release these hidden thought patterns, your desire and willingness to make a change is absolutely vital.

By using your relationship toolkit you gain new options: you can make the choice to change and grow with your new thoughts; or, to stay comfortable in the repetitive outcomes your old thoughts create. As long as you are consciously making a choice, you are in charge of your destiny.

Because I believe actions speak louder than words, I am going to share with you an example of how changing your old beliefs to *New Thoughts* works. The example is about a single woman named Betty who wants to attract her ideal partner.

Betty is a popular single woman who attracts many men. Every time she starts dating someone special, her old lover named Jerry calls her. Jerry acts so sweet and understanding that Betty wants him.

However, sweet as Jerry is, Betty despises Jerry for dangling in front of her the carrot of a long-term relationship. He will not commit to Betty's request that they share a long-term relationship. Jerry's behaviour confuses Betty. Part of Betty wants Jerry, while another part despises him.

Betty and Jerry are interesting because both of them are suffering pain. At the moment, however, their pain is acceptable because it provides a way for them to continue their fear of intimacy at a subconscious level. Once they become aware of how their pain is serving them to avoid intimacy, they can make changes. They can choose:

1. To share their new awareness and work together to achieve intimacy, or

2. To separate and move on to new situations that resonate with their desires.

Issues such as *fear of intimacy* are what I refer to as *Relationship Barriers*. As the example illustrates, breaking through relationship barriers is a choice. Making a conscious decision to either change to a *New Thought,* or to stay in your old habit pattern of beliefs, is a choice.

Deciding to change your old habit patterns (core beliefs) takes courage and willingness.

As far as being happy, what matters is that you respect your choice. When you consciously choose your relationship experiences, you can expect your self-confidence to grow and your ability to deal with your fears to be far greater. You will be able to perceive problems not as obstacles, but rather as opportunities for growth and shaping your relationship to give you exactly what you desire. Keeping this in mind, the most important thing you can do for yourself as you learn how to change old habit patterns to *New Thoughts* is to have fun. You can even turn it into a game. You can have fun watching the results and returning to your inner negotiating table when you want to make alterations.

Relationship issues represent all those reasons why you *can't, won't and are not* enjoying a satisfying, fulfilling relationship. The reasons (causes) may be buried in your subconscious thinking so you may not be aware of them. If you are having difficulty making and keeping a commitment to achieve a loving, lasting relationship, or are unhappy in a long-term relationship, this is an excellent indication that you are up against a barrier of relationship issues.

AN IMPORTANT REMINDER: The greater your fear, the greater your resistance to change. The greater your resistance to change, the harder you must work to maintain your relationship barriers (issues). With a willing attitude to move through your fears and to change, your *Trusted Relationship Tools* will guide you in making your relationship dreams come true. It is your simple guide to **"How To Find True Love."**

Replacing Old Belief Patterns With New Thoughts

My Pocket-sized Relationship Toolkit

To grow and shape your loving relationships you need *know-how.* You need options of what you can do to overcome obstacles - to grow and shape your relationship. To make this possible, I am providing you with this *proven pocket-sized relationship toolkit* . It is yours to keep! When you are up against relationship issues you desire to change, repeat your *New Thought* several times daily. For best results, I suggest you write out your *New Thought* on a 3 X 5-inch index card and stick it somewhere handy such as on your bathroom mirror, on your car dashboard, or by your bedside.

Continue repeating your *New Thought* until it replaces your old belief, and you are experiencing a positive change in your relationship.

Normally this takes six weeks; however, when your desire is high and you are enthusiastic, change happens more rapidly. In many proven cases, change has taken place instantly. What is important is that you repeat your *New Thoughts* until they become new habits automatically triggering your success.

There are more than fifty relationship issues (barriers) that I have identified. The *New Thoughts* that I have selected to overcome and replace the old belief patterns have been tested and proven in several groups over a period of twenty *plus* years. As you browse through the relationship barriers, you will be attracted to those that promise to make a difference in your relationship. Notice if a pattern arises in the barriers you have selected.

In your ***Trusted Toolkit*** that follows, each relationship barrier is identified by the belief that creates and sustains the barrier.

REMEMBER: *The way to change a relationship barrier is to repeat the New Thought until it becomes habit and you notice a positive change in your relationship.*

50 PLUS RELATIONSHIP BARRIERS AND YOUR TOOLS FOR OVERCOMING THEM

ABANDONMENT

BELIEF: I have been rejected and left out. I feel betrayed, fearful, and hurt. It is hard for me to trust again.

NEW THOUGHT: I let go of feeling rejected and replace my feelings with understanding, compassion and forgiveness. I am open to understanding my pain, what thoughts I had to cause my pain, and to forgive myself and everyone involved in abandoning me. I am thankful for all I have including *Who I Am*. As Spirit, I am *Love Power* and have all that I need to create a fulfilling relationship.

ACKNOWLEDGEMENT

BELIEF: I am not being acknowledged for the good I do. No matter what I do, I can't seem to please my partner. I am a failure - no good!

NEW THOUGHT: I acknowledge my own worth. The more I love myself, the easier it is for other people to accept, acknowledge and appreciate the good things I do.

ABUSE

BELIEF: I am not lovable. Whenever I get interested in someone who I think is special, that person starts using and hurting me. I need to protect myself from being hurt. Sometimes I am fearful for my safety.

NEW THOUGHT: I am loveable. Right *NOW*, I stop being a victim! It is my right to say what I want and to express my feelings. It is as easy to say *no* as it is to say *yes*. I say *no* whenever I need to stop someone from abusing me. I deserve to be listened to and heard. I am worthwhile. I choose not to be an enabler to someone who tries to abuse me; e.g, my partner.

ADDICTION

BELIEF: I rely on quick fixes (for example: alcohol, drugs, cigarettes, food, sex, excessive work, power and money, an inflated ego, feeling sorry for myself) to give me courage to handle my problems. Using quick fixes, I am able to endure my pain and fool myself into believing that everything is okay.

NEW THOUGHT: Here and now, I declare I am in control. When I feel an addictive craving coming on, I tell myself to *STOP* what I am thinking and *CALM DOWN*.

I focus my attention into a place of inner peace. From this place of inner peace, I create a step-by-step plan of action to guide me into new addictive-free experiences. I do whatever it takes to become the master of my thoughts and emotions.

AGE, COLOR, SEXUAL ORIENTATION, RELI-GION, ATTRACTIVENESS

BELIEF: I am not good enough for a loving, lasting relationship so it won't work. I have one of these obstacles: not the right age (too big an age difference), not the right color, not the right sexual orientation, not the right religion, or not attractive enough. The relationship I want is destined to fail.

NEW THOUGHT: Love has no boundaries. As Kahlil Gibran says in *The Prophet*, "Love if it finds you worthy, directs your course." *Love Power* overcomes every obstacle. I am worthy of a loving, lasting relationship and have faith it will work.

ANGER:

BELIEF: I am disgusted and prone to feelings of hate and even rage. I can't control what is happening. I blame other people, the situation, God, and fate. Deep down I am angry with myself because I do not know how to handle the situation.

NEW THOUGHT: I release and let go of my anger and other negative feelings by:

1. daily acknowledging the presence of my *Love Power*, and then breathing deeply into a feeling of calm where I can change my thoughts and feelings,

2. *channeling my anger into an opportunity for positive inspiration and growth,*

3. *listening to the messages my anger gives me so I can change the way I perceive what is happening,*

4. *deliberately returning to love and trusting my Love Power.*

ANXIETY/PERFORMANCE

BELIEF: I am overwhelmed by the thought of having to achieve my goals. They seem huge, and I fear I will be rejected if I don't accomplish them. I won't share my fears with my partner because I would appear weak and inadequate. I'll keep my performance anxiety to myself.

NEW THOUGHT: I deliberately move into a feeling of inner peace, awaken my *LOVE POWER*, and in the peace become mindful of my worthiness. Then, from a place of inner peace and worthiness, I break down my goals into small, achievable steps focusing on one step at a time. I share my hopes and fears with my partner. I accept and value myself for Who I Am.

ATTACHMENT

BELIEF: I am not able to separate my own worthiness from that of my partner. I am powerless to separate my own feelings and to express myself. I am easily hurt and defensive.

NEW THOUGHT: I emotionally stand out of the shadow of my partner and breathe deeply until I experience a calm sense of control and peace. This accomplished, I acknowledge my own abilities and strengths. I continue this practice until I am okay with or without my partner. I choose to be myself, to remember that I am important and that it is my responsibility to create my own happiness. The more fulfilled I am, the more love I have to share with my partner.

BEING BETRAYED

BELIEF: I am being betrayed and lied to. I hurt and don't like it.

NEW THOUGHT: Intentionally I forgive and move beyond the lie and any feelings of hurt and rejection.

Instead, I reflect upon what I was thinking and doing that attracted my partner to betray me. I am willing to move into my *LOVE POWER* and change my thoughts to attract love, respect, and acceptance.

BETRAYING OTHERS

BELIEF: I am not keeping my word. This way I am safe.

NEW THOUGHT: My word is my pledge and is sacred. Being truthful with my partner sets me free.

BEING CHEATED

BELIEF: My partner is either seeing someone else behind my back or doing something about which I do not know and would disapprove. I can't trust my partner.

NEW THOUGHT: I openly share my thoughts and feelings with my partner, and am willing to understand my partner's thoughts and feelings. With compassion and good communication, we can resolve our issues. I faithfully do my *Love Communication* exercises.

BORED

BELIEF: My relationship with my partner is always the same – or, at least some part of it, is definitely boring. I must silently grin and bear the situation. There is nothing I can do to create excitement.

NEW THOUGHT: I open myself up to experiencing new things with or without my partner. I replace awkwardness, fear and perhaps shame with excitement and adventure. When stuck, I reach out and ask my partner for help. Being honest with my partner is my best tool.

BULLYING AND HURTING OTHERS

BELIEF: Bullying and hurting others is an effective way for me to be respected and get what I want. At a deep inner level bullying and hurting others helps me hide my own fears that I am not good enough and am not loved or loveable.

NEW THOUGHT: By believing in myself and embracing my *Love Power*, I can get what I want and be respected. I love and accept myself for Who I Am. Love, gratitude, and kindness are effective ways of getting what I want and building a mutually fulfilling relationship. The only people who hurt are those people willing to be hurt. I can't make anyone hurt.

CHEATING ON MY PARTNER

BELIEF: I am cheating and being dishonest with my partner. Cheating is okay as long as I am not caught. Even if I want to stop, I can't.

NEW THOUGHT: I have the strength and *Love Power* to be faithful and honest with my partner. Being honest and willing to forgive one another sets us both free.

COMMITMENT

BELIEF: I fear commitment. What if I pledge to love someone, and then my dreams are not fulfilled? I could end up being a prisoner in a relationship that I no longer want.

NEW THOUGHT: When I commit to a relationship, I choose to believe it will work. My pledge creates passion and is the driving Love force of our intimacy. With commitment, I gain freedom to share whom I am in an intimate relationship in which we both grow and prosper.

To achieve a relationship in which we both grow, I honour and respect myself and my partner for w*hom we are.* As a way to nourish our self-growth, I express my thoughts and feelings and lovingly listen to my partner. Whenever I experience we are not in harmony, I choose to communicate my concerns until we both return to feeling loved.

Fear is the lack of knowledge. With understanding and embracing my *Love Power*, fear disappears.

COMPETITIVE

BELIEF: I will make it look as though I am as good as, or better than, anyone else. When my *fake me* is believed by others, I will relax. Nobody can love the *real me.*

NEW THOUGHT: I am worthwhile. By sharing our strengths and weaknesses, my partner and I are okay to make mistakes. We trust we will continue to be loved for our r*eal selves.*

COMPLAINING

BELIEF: I can't get what I want unless I complain about what I don't like. My opinions matter.

NEW THOUGHT: By trusting my partner to listen to my desires, I get what I want. I focus positively on the future and ask for what I want. I make my requests reasonable, specific and something that I believe my partner can do.

CON ARTIST

BELIEF: If I tell my partner what he/she wants to hear, I can seduce my partner into getting what I want without having to reveal my own inadequacies. I fear telling my partner the truth.

NEW THOUGHT: Being honest with my partner sets me free. The more I love and trust myself, the more I am able to love and trust my partner. I am *Love Power* and I am worthwhile.

DEFENSIVE/OVERBEARING/CONFRONTIVE

BELIEF: Reacting defensively and confronting others, I create a protective shield around me. This protects me from other people putting me down and from being a victim. It also makes me appear powerful. People would not like me if they knew the *real me.*

NEW THOUGHT: I am okay just the way I am. Other people's petty criticisms of me are a projection of who they are and have nothing to do with whom I am. I listen patiently to loving, constructive observations and expect my comments to be respectfully heard. I am filled with confidence. My *Love Power* sees me through.

DESERVING/INADEQUATE

BELIEF: I don't deserve an intimate lasting relationship. I am not worthy. Ultimately I ruin all my promising intimate relationships.

NEW THOUGHT: I deserve to be loved and to share an intimate lasting relationship. I am willing to work on all aspects of myself that I believe would not make me a good partner (e.g. a drug- related addiction, anger issues, low self-esteem). Deep down I know I am worthwhile. I love myself and am willing to receive. I am willing to share with my partner and go the extra mile to make our relationship work. Together we will let our *Love Power* shine.

DISAPPOINTMENT

BELIEF: I feel badly that what I want and expect in my relationship is not working. My partner is not doing what I want and what I believe is best for both of us.

NEW THOUGHT: I am willing to forgive and forget what doesn't work thus making room for what will work. With a loving attitude, I change my expectations and appreciate my partner for who he/she is. I trust we can overcome any obstacle by using our Love Power and communication tools wisely.

EMBARRASSED

BELIEF: I feel self-conscious and awkward exposing my thoughts and feelings.

NEW THOUGHT: It is okay to be vulnerable and to make mistakes. I love and trust myself. Being truthful with my partner sets us both free to be genuine and truly loved for who we are.

EMOTIONAL SHUT-DOWN

BELIEF: Not revealing my feelings enables me to be safe and avoid being hurt. Deep down I fear my attempts to get close will fail.

NEW THOUGHT: Sharing my thoughts and feelings with my partner brings us closer together. I choose to open my heart and trust the guidance of my Love Power to keep me safe.

FEAR

BELIEF: I place my faith in that which appears real, and then believe the worst could happen. Scared, I surrender my personal power to conditions outside myself that give me a false (fake) sense of security.

NEW THOUGHT: There is no barrier, no fears that our *Love Power* will not dissolve. With an open heart and mind, I embrace an attitude of love and gratitude. The light that shines forth from my *Love Power* casts out the dark shadows of fear until fear disappears. Love is the absence of fear. Fear is only a thought appearing real but has absolutely no validity - has no substance and is not real.

FORGIVENESS

You make what you defend against, and by your own defence against it, it is real and inescapable. Lay down your arms, and only then do you perceive it false. A Course in Miracles

BELIEF: I blame myself and sometimes others rather

than forgiving. I act out of feelings of regret, hurt, anger, shame, guilt and remorse.

NEW THOUGHT: I forgive and choose thoughts that empower me to respect and appreciate myself and others. I am my own best friend. Everything I need to achieve satisfying relationships is within me. I am guided by and with my *Love Power.*

FRUSTRATION

BELIEF: I am blocked. I can't get what I want in my relationship. I feel like the saying, "I am damned if I do, and damned if I don't"

NEW THOUGHT: Being frustrated is okay because it motivates me to explore new solutions. When blocked, I like sharing my thoughts and feelings with my partner who is willing to listen and support me. I enjoy replacing worry, frustration and struggle with excitement to learn more and to grow. I trust my *Love Power.*

GUILT

BELIEF: I don't feel good about what I have done. It is my fault. I have violated my own code of ethics.

NEW THOUGHT: I forgive myself and release myself from feelings of guilt. By changing my thoughts, I change my experiences. The mistakes I make do not matter, but what I do to correct them does matter. I use my mistakes as creative opportunities for building a more healthy and fulfilling relationship.

HEALTH CONCERNS

BELIEF: My health is poor. I don't want to be a burden.

NEW THOUGHT: I am a Divine Spiritual Being having a human experience. My body is my intimate friend. I treat my body with respect. My thoughts create my experiences including my body, and not visa-versa. I *know* every day my health grows stronger.

HURTING/ FEAR OF BEING HURT

BELIEF: I have been hurt before and fear being hurt again. I am powerless and unable to defend myself against being hurt.

NEW THOUGHT: No one can hurt me unless I give them permission and accept being hurt. The more I love myself, the more my partner and other people are able to love me. I am willing to receive love. The past is gone, and every moment is a new opportunity to choose my thoughts and feelings wisely thus creating a new reality/ realization. Thank you, *Love Power*!

HYPOCHONDRIAC

BELIEF: I worry about my health. I have no control over my health. I am limited by the belief that I have many physical ailments.

NEW THOUGHT: I am worthwhile. My body is my intimate friend and messenger. Thoughts are things and give me control over my health. My thoughts create my future including what happens in my body. I trust my *Love Power* to guide me in choosing thoughts that are good for my health.

INTELLECTUALIZING

BELIEF: I use my knowledge to create a rational defence that protects me from exposing my inadequacies and the possibility of being wrong. Deep down, I fear being exposed and rejected.

NEW THOUGHT: I am worthwhile. I let go of trying to protect myself from having to be right and instead trust in my Spiritual Essence to guide me. Sharing my real thoughts and feelings with my partner sets me free.

INTIMACY

BELIEF: I fear getting emotionally close and revealing my true thoughts and feelings. I don't want to be rejected, or to lose my freedom and feel useless.

NEW THOUGHT: My relationships mirror whom I am. By sharing an intimate relationship with my partner, we discover more about ourselves. This is an exciting adventure and grows the strength and beauty of who we are individually and as a couple. Love is the strongest force in the universe and I can use my *Love Power* to maintain a healthy, vibrant intimacy. Being truthful with my partner sets me free to deepen and expand our intimacy.

JEALOUSY

BELIEF: My partner is mine and I expect my partner to be there exclusively for me. I am jealous and feel rage when my partner shows affection for someone else. Deep down, I am afraid my partner will leave me.

NEW THOUGHT: I believe I am worth loving and have the power to create what is best for me. If my partner were to choose someone else, I would honor my partner's decision. I would have faith that someone or something better for me would fill my emotional vacuum. I replace jealousy with love of myself, trust, and compassion.

JUDGEMENTAL/CRITICAL

BELIEF: What I believe is right. Usually I know what works and is good for other people including for my partner. It is my responsibility to set things right.

NEW THOUGHT: I am willing to see that what is right for me is often not what is right for other people including for my partner. As I focus on my partner's good qualities, we expand our understanding and appreciation of each other.

LONELINESS

BELIEF: I feel sad and empty being alone. I believe I am not worthy of being loved and am destined to remain alone. I experience deep loss in my lack of companionship.

NEW THOUGHT: Being alone provides me with an opportunity for self-discovery and to do things I could not do while being with a partner. I bless my alone time and being able to discover what I want in a lasting, intimate relationship. I move forward with confidence *knowing* I will attract my ideal relationship. I will make a list of all the attributes I desire and deserve (become the living compliment of what I am requesting), and put my request out to the law of the Universe *knowing* my ideal partner will be attracted to me.

LOSS

BELIEF: My relationships end up in loss due to death, divorce, rejection and/or abandonment. I fear being out of control and suffering emotional pain.

NEW THOUGHT: Loss is a reaction to experiences, and I no longer choose this reaction. Instead I choose thoughts of health, happiness and fulfilling relationships. I trust in a power of peace and love greater than myself to deliver what is best for me. I remember that my *Love Power* is part of the greatest force in the universe, and I can use it to attract a loving, lasting relationship.

MARRIAGE

BELIEF: Marriage is a romantic fairy tale of unrealistic expectations that don't come true. In my marriage, I feel like the romance has died and I am stuck in a relationship where I can't get what I want. I have lost my freedom, don't know what to do - am afraid of leaving. More than a third of marriages are either failing or not fulfilling.

NEW THOUGHT: I believe that love is the strongest force in the universe and that we can use Love Power. Using Love Power and good communication skills, my partner and I can make choices that are mutually fulfilling, enrich our lives, and bring us happiness. I focus on the large percentage of marriages that do succeed.

MATERIALISTIC

BELIEF: Money and material possessions give me power, prestige, and respect.

NEW THOUGHT: My happiness is being valued for whom I am. I open my heart and accept my inner peace as my power. This *Love Power* is the source and substance of my good experiences.

NARCISSISTIC/EGO DRIVEN

BELIEF: I am important, superior and deserve special recognition and treatment. When I don't get treated with special attention and loyalty, it is my job to criticize and belittle others like my partner. This way whomever I choose to criticize and belittle such as my partner can remember who is superior and whom they are serving. All people and events are an extension of me. I love myself and the world revolves around me.

NEW THOUGHT: I recognize that other people are separate from me and are important and special. I reach out to others including my partner with understanding and recognize that I have a problem with insecurity. I focus on building a healthy self-image. I put my faith and trust in a divine power greater than myself. I believe other people like my partner are there for me, and I am open to receiving their help.

OVERPROTECTIVE

BELIEF: My partner does not know what he/she is doing. I'll take care of my partner and protect him/her from potential harm. Deep down, I am afraid that if my partner does not need me, I will be abandoned.

NEW THOUGHT: I am worthwhile. The more freedom I give my partner, the more freedom I receive. By trusting my partner and knowing my partner can take care of him/her self, I gain respect and deepen our intimacy.

OVERWHELMED

BELIEF: I feel out of control – swept up in a wave of pressure. I can't stay focused on doing what I want and don't believe my partner can, or will, help me. I keep making mistakes, am anxious, and fear our relationship is headed for disaster.

NEW THOUGHT: I do whatever it takes to relax. In a relaxed state I connect with my *Love Power*, Divine Essence, and ask Spirit to guide me - I am open to receiving and that includes help from my partner and other people. With trust and an open heart, I make plans breaking them into small manageable steps.

PAINFUL

BELIEF: Either I am in pain, or I can't stand to see my partner suffer. I can't figure out how to ask my partner for help and am not sure my partner would help if I asked. I feel helpless. The only way I know how to manage my pain is to avoid the sad situation.

NEW THOUGHT: There is no obstacle that enough *Love Power* can not overcome. By sharing with my partner and using professional skills if needed, we can heal any painful situation.

Working together we deepen our understanding and intimacy. I choose to focus on a positive outcome, and to visualize myself and my partner in physical and Emotional Well Being.

PLEASING MY PARTNER

BELIEF: I must do everything I can to please my partner or I won't be loved. Even if I have to go into sacrifice, I must please my partner.

NEW THOUGHT: Pleasing myself is as important as pleasing my partner. Together my partner and I share our intimate thoughts and feelings with the intention of both of us being pleased, happy and growing our relationship. We use our *Love Power* to guide us. We are grateful for our loving relationship, and all the blessings we have to share.

POWER STRUGGLE

BELIEF: I need to know I have power and to be in control of what happens in our relationship. It is important for me to be right. I need to defend myself as my partner tries to take control and win at being right.

NEW THOUGHT: I am powerful and get to choose how I use my power. Rather than trying to control what happens in our relationship and be right, I use my LOVE POWER and my communication skills to discover what my partner means – not just what my partner is saying. The more I love and appreciate my partner, the more I love and appreciate myself. I enjoy being an active partner in enhancing our intimacy.

PROCRASTINATION/EXCUSES

BELIEF: If I put off doing what I know I should do, I won't have to risk suffering unwanted consequences such as failure or more success than I can handle. By procrastinating, I can avoid taking responsibility for what happens. The thought of taking action is overwhelming.

NEW THOUGHT: As an individualized expression of the Divine, I exercise my God-given power of volition in choosing what to do, when, where, and how. I enjoy taking small, incremental steps toward fulfillment. As I feel good about what I am doing, I attract successful experiences to me.

REJECTION

BELIEF: If I express my real thoughts and feelings, other people (including my partner) will reject me. I'll be abandoned, alone, and suffer pain in my loneliness. My dreams will be shattered.

NEW THOUGHT: I am worthwhile and worthy. Expressing my real thoughts and feelings attracts people (including my partner) who appreciate me for whom I am. I replace fear of being rejected with trust that I am worthwhile and provided for. When I am alone, I have the time to deepen and clarify what I truly want.

RESENTMENT

BELIEF: I am indignant and upset about what my partner is doing. I don't believe my partner wants to hear about what is upsetting me. Because I can't change what is happening, I have to put up with it. I will keep my anger to myself even though I know it is unhealthy to repress emotions.

NEW THOUGHT: I am in charge of my feelings and what happens to me. By trusting my partner, I can better understand the situation. I know my partner is willing to listen to my feelings. When we put love and our relationship first, we can share our thoughts and feelings and overcome any obstacle. We faithfully use our *Love Communication* knowledge and exercises.

RISK TAKING

BELIEF: I am afraid to risk taking action to better our relationship because deep down I fear that I will fail. If I fail, my partner may reject me and even leave me. I don't want to suffer hurting or being alone.

NEW THOUGHT: Love is letting go of fear. I am willing to use the power of love, *LOVE POWER,* to take risks and move through personal barriers. I am in control of my thoughts. By using my thoughts correctly, I create what happens in my relationship including creating a loving intimacy.

ROLE EXPECTATIONS

BELIEF: My parents, peers, and culture taught me that men and women are supposed to act in certain ways. For example, men are supposed to be the performers and breadwinners, and women are supposed to be the house-keepers and manage the relationship. Men are expected to be strong and assertive, and women to be vulnerable and express their feelings. When I either *can't* or *don't* meet the male/female role expectations, I feel like a failure. I'm confused and frustrated.

NEW THOUGHT: It's okay to be different. I love myself just the way I am. Sharing my beliefs and feelings with my partner empowers my partner to love me for who I am.

"*When men and women are able to respect and accept their differences then love has a chance to blossom.*" —John Gray, "Men Are From Mars, *Women are From Venus*"

SAD/SORROWFUL

BELIEF: I feel sad things did not turn out as I believe they should have. Unfortunately, there is nothing I can do about it. Sometimes I feel sad for other people, and sometimes I feel sad for myself.

NEW THOUGHT: I release myself from trying and judging the way things turned out. I accept that I can't change the past. I am worthy, powerful, and have the ability to make changes. My experiences provide me with an orderly sequence of learning and growth. As I focus on the present and future, I am 100% in charge of my present and future experiences.

SELF SACRIFICE

BELIEF: I must constantly give to my partner even if I am uncomfortable and sacrificing my own needs and desires. If I don't give enough, I will be criticized, rejected and jeopardize our intimacy.

NEW THOUGHT: Sharing what I need and desire with my partner frees me up to be myself and to receive. The more love I give, the more love I have to receive. When both my partner and I are happy, we unleash the power of our passion to bring us what we want joyously and to enjoy an authentic, trusting relationship.

SEX

BELIEF (For Men): If I do not perform well, I won't be loved by my partner. If my friends find out, they may laugh at me. Even at the expense of denying my own needs, I must please my partner.

BELIEF (For Women): If I don't act like I am happy and satisfied by my partner's lovemaking, I will lose his love and affection.

NEW THOUGHT: Sex is one way I express my intimate love for my partner. Sharing both my fears and desires with my partner opens our hearts to be loved for who we are. I am patient, listen to what my partner wants, and am willing to explore new ways of sexual expression and making love.

SHAME

BELIEF: I or someone I know has intentionally broken a moral code of ethics and done something dishonorable, improper or hurtful. Being consciously aware of the event and what was happening, I suffer the pain of humiliation and embarrassment.

NEW THOUGHT: In my heart, I know I am a good person. I forgive myself for my mistakes and forgive others for judging me. I move forward with kindness, confidence and a positive attitude.

SHY

BELIEF: Relationships are stressful and awkward for me in some situations. This includes the initial conversation, keeping the conversation going, expressing my feelings, and in romance and sexuality. I feel inadequate and sometimes lack education. Deep down I do not feel worthy and believe I can easily be rejected.

NEW THOUGHT: I am worthwhile and loveable just the way I am. It is okay for me to ask for and receive help. Being truthful and asking questions puts my partner at ease and opens us up to share our strengths and weaknesses. Through open sharing and honesty, we deepen our intimacy.

STRESS

BELIEF: Mine or my partner's demands are more than I can handle. It is hard to stay in control. Often I feel anxious, irritable, pressured, sick, depressed and tired.

NEW THOUGHT: A little stress motivates me. High stress controls me. When I experience high stress, I take a relaxation break. I relax until I experience a sense of inner peace that intuitively lets me know I am okay and effectively choosing what to do. I am willing to break down my "to-do" lists into smaller steps, to ask for help (including asking my partner), to use prayer, and also to use relaxation methods such as yoga and meditation.

STUBBORN

BELIEF: I am not going to listen to what my partner says. I'm not budging from my beliefs. No one can make me do what I don't want to do.

NEW THOUGHT: My partner and I are part of a larger spiritual whole. As I give to my partner, my partner is better equipped to please me. As I listen to my partner, I learn more about myself. I am willing to do whatever it takes to nourish our love and intimacy.

STUCKNESS

BELIEF: I am stuck in a repetitious pattern (such as rejection, addiction or abuse), and I can't get out.

NEW THOUGHT: Can't is another way of saying *I don't know how.* I open myself up to learning how to release myself from my stuck pattern – I am open to changing my thoughts, to meditation and prayer, to helpful information, and to professional coaching. I am patient and know a change in my thoughts/beliefs will change my experiences.

SUFFOCATING

BELIEF: I feel like life is slipping away from me and I am suffocating. I'm losing my identity and must sacrifice my beliefs to please and be loved. I lack faith in my own values and power.

NEW THOUGHT: Being stuck motivates me to re-examine my thoughts, beliefs, and values. I refocus my thoughts from what I don't have to thoughts of gratitude for what I do have. I have faith that gratitude opens the doors for new and wonderful experiences to be attracted to me.

In an attitude of gratitude, I give thanks for the following: "I am the source. I am the power. I am worthwhile and willing to express my beliefs. It is as easy to say *No* as it is to say *Yes.*"

TAKING YOUR PARTNER FOR GRANTED

BELIEF: (Please be aware that this belief is often held unconsciously.) Because my partner needs our relationship, I do not have to fear my partner leaving me. By satisfying my partner's basic requirements, I am free to concentrate on other things I want.

NEW THOUGHT: As I listen to my partner's needs, it is easier to understand and appreciate my partner and myself. Through sharing we create more freedom to live an authentic relationship in which we are free, mutually respected, and grow stronger. Focusing on my partner's good qualities expands our love. I enjoy sharing my intimate thoughts and feelings with my partner.

WITHDRAWAL

BELIEF: Withdrawing is my way of demonstrating my resignation and silently retaliating. I can appear mature and in control thus hiding my real anger and inability to know how to safely express myself.

NEW THOUGHT: I remember that I am LOVE POWER. Then, with calm courage, I forgive and reach out to understand my partner and the real meaning of what my partner is saying. To create an atmosphere of caring and safety, I find something my partner is doing that I like. In a safe and caring atmosphere, we use our communication skills. The more we share, the stronger our love and intimacy becomes.

About the Author

For seventeen years in Vancouver, BC, Canada, Blenda enjoyed the private practice of Professional Clinical Therapy. Specializing in relationships, Blenda successfully worked with more than 6,500 clients. She brought into Canada the work of the renowned bestselling relationship author, Dr. John Gray and co-facilitated his relationship workshops. Later Dr. John Gray endorsed Blenda's book called **LOVE SECRETS,** *Falling in Love & Staying in Love.* He said "This book is a practical and compassionate guide for creating healthy and lasting intimacy."

Having a strong interest in metaphysics, Blenda also became a minister. As Blenda says, "What brings me the greatest satisfaction in my relationship work is seeing individuals realize they are worthy of love and being loved. By using your Love Power in combination with the relationship tools contained in **How to get True Love**, you can enjoy the best relationship imaginable!"

Made in the USA
Columbia, SC
25 June 2018